NTC SKILL BUILDERS

WHAT YOU NEED TO KNOW ABOUT
DEVELOPING YOUR TEST-TAKING SKILLS: READING COMPREHENSION

Robert S. Boone

DATE DUE

Printed on recyclable paper

VGM Career Horizons
a division of *NTC Publishing Group*
Lincolnwood, Illinois USA

For permission to use copyrighted material, grateful thanks are given
to the copyright holders listed below.
page 76, "O World" by George Santayana. Reprinted by permission of
The MIT Press.
page 78, "What Mystery Pervades a Well!" Reprinted by permission
of the publishers and the Trustees of Amherst College from THE POEMS
OF EMILY DICKINSON, Thomas H. Johnson, ed., Cambridge, Mass.:
The Belknap Press of Harvard University Press, Copyright © 1951,
1955, 1979, 1983 by the President and Fellows of Harvard College.

5 6 7 8 9 VP 0 9 8 7 6 5 4 3 2 1

Contents

READINGS IN HUMANITIES   63

Reading Comprehension

Readings in Social Studies

Readings in Science

Readings in Humanities

INTRODUCTION

In the high-tech world we live in today, just how important is the ability to read? Has the readily accessible information highway diminished the need to read well?

Far from it. The ability to read and to comprehend what one has read is no less important now than it was previously. In fact, college admissions and employment opportunities may depend upon strong scores on reading tests.

The importance placed upon the ability to read with understanding is also evident in tests such as the ACT and the SAT. For example, the SAT now includes longer readings and more challenging questions. The ACT has adopted a broader range of reading selections, adding literature passages to the traditional mix of natural science and social studies.

What, then, is the key to performing well on a reading test? Your test results will depend upon *how* you read, and the simple three-step strategy shown in this book can help you read more effectively. You should begin by recognizing that reading with understanding and sensitivity is not a passive activity. Rather, it requires your full attention and concentrated effort to employ the reading strategies discussed in the pages that follow. Fortunately, your efforts to improve your reading ability in preparation for tests such as the ACT and the SAT will serve you well both at school and in the workplace.

THREE STEPS TO STRATEGIC READING

Is having a reading strategy really necessary? Admittedly, you probably won't need to apply this strategy when reading a paperback mystery by your favorite author, but that's because reading a mystery for pleasure requires less effort than other kinds of reading you'll be asked to do. Indeed, reading a complex description of photosynthesis or a detailed legal contract is best done using a strategy such as the following:

1. Preview before you read.
2. Underline and annotate while you read.
3. Summarize after you read.

Preview

When you read material on unfamiliar subjects—such as those you are likely to encounter on reading tests—you need to equip yourself to understand what you are reading. In these circumstances, previewing is a useful beginning strategy because it helps you to gain an overview of the material and to anticipate the topics addressed in it.

Instead of starting at the beginning and reading through carefully, your goal is to take in the entire passage at once. Begin by asking yourself what you think the passage contains. Study the title, the first paragraph, the last sentence of the first paragraph, the topic sentences, and any italicized words. And, of course, read the discussion questions that follow the passage, because they will tend to touch on the more important ideas considered. Then answer these questions:

- What is the subject of the passage?
- What point is the author making about this subject?

Ultimately, this previewing process will save you time. And even if your guess about the content of the passage is incorrect, you have gained in the process of previewing. The preview, though brief, has given you expectations about the content of the material. Like a scientist testing a hypothesis, you are focused on the outcome, that is, the accuracy of your expectations about the content of the passage.

Underline and Annotate

The second step of the reading strategy—underline and annotate—happens *as* you read. The purpose is to keep you alert and fully involved in the material you are reading. Becoming a participant prevents you from slipping into the bad habits of an unfocused, passive reader.

As you read, what should you be looking for to underline or annotate? You should underline

- topic sentences
- key words
- unfamiliar words
- passages that relate specifically to the questions that follow the reading material

You should jot notes in the margins regarding main ideas. Some students do more underlining and annotating than others, but the point is to use your pen to mark a path through complex or difficult reading. At the very least, the active process of writing comments and underlining important concepts keeps you alert and focused on the reading passage.

Note: You should never write in a book that does not belong to you.

Summarize

Summarizing is the final step of the reading strategy. Always try to write a short summary of what you have read. Not only will this serve to help you recall the passage as a whole, you will quickly identify any sections that you don't quite understand. Don't get bogged down in writing, though. There is no need to make your summary longer than a few sentences; however, do be certain to include in your summary the answers to the questions you considered earlier in the previewing step:

- What is the subject of the passage?
- What point is the author making about this subject?

Without question, you will find the three-step reading strategy of preview, underline and annotate, and summarize to be highly useful for all of your school work. In fact, many successful students write short summaries after each paragraph in a detailed or difficult chapter. Though you might find this practice to be somewhat tedious at first, your investment of time will pay big benefits when you turn to your notes to help you review for an exam.

Beyond the strategic reading practice you gain by using this text, there are additional techniques you can use to help you read more actively. For example, read for pleasure daily. At the end of each day's reading, write a brief summary. Newspaper articles afford the same opportunities to read strategically. Finally, choose some reading material and make up a test for it. Use a format like the one employed in this book. Focus your questions on main idea and technical devices the author used.

PRACTICING STRATEGIC READING

Following are different forms of writing that often appear on standardized tests. Practice previewing, underlining and annotating, and summarizing as you read. As on the tests, this collection includes a variety of subjects, including social studies, science, and humanities. In almost every instance, the author of the passage is a famous writer such as Edgar Allan Poe, Emily Dickinson, or Thomas Paine—individuals who have set standards for excellence in writing.

Each selection will begin with a prompt. The purpose of the prompt is to encourage you to focus briefly on the issues the passage raises before you begin to read. Following the reading itself, you will find a space with the heading *Preview*. Make sure, *before* you read the passage, to write a quick description of what you think the reading will cover. Then, after you have completed your reading of the passage, write a short summary of what you have read. Finally, answer the questions provided to help you assess your understanding of the passage.

Readings in Social Studies

SOME GUIDELINES

Following is a collection of reading passages devoted to social studies. Note the techniques these authors use to present factual information, to argue, and to persuade. These passages are commentaries on society, on humankind, and on government.

Each passage is followed by questions that center on the following key areas:

- The central point
- The details and examples supporting the central point
- Information that can be inferred from the passage
- Aspects of writing that the passage illustrates

Pay attention to the *kinds* of questions that are asked. You can expect to encounter questions with a similar focus on the ACT and other standard tests. Remember to read all of the choices and to choose the *best* answer to the question.

Remember to practice the three steps to strategic reading:

1. Preview before you read.
2. Underline and annotate while you read.
3. Summarize after you read.

From "Walking," Henry David Thoreau

Prompt: Recall a time that you lived too much in the past. Can we think too much about the future?

Above all, we cannot afford not to live in the present. He is blessed over all mortals who loses no moment of the passing life in remembering the past. Unless our philosophy hears the cock crow in every barnyard within our horizon, it is belated. That sound commonly reminds us that we are growing rusty and antique in our employments and habits of thought. His philosophy comes down to a more recent time than ours. There is something suggested by it that is a newer testament—the gospel according to this moment. He has not fallen astern; he has got up early and kept up early, and to be where he is is to be in season, in the foremost rank of time. It is an expression of the health and soundness of Nature, a brag for all the world—healthiness as of a spring burst forth, a new fountain of the Muses, to celebrate this last instant of time. Where he lives no fugitive slave laws are passed. Who has not betrayed his master many times since last he heard that note?

The merit of this bird's strain is in its freedom from all plaintiveness. The singer can easily move us to tears or to laughter, but where is he who can excite in us a pure morning joy? When, in doleful dumps, breaking the awful stillness of our wooden sidewalk on a Sunday, or, perchance, a watcher in the house of mourning, I hear a cockerel crow far or near, I think to myself, "There is one of us well, at any rate," and with a sudden gush return to my senses.

Preview the passage to gain an overview. Then write your answers to the following questions:

- What is the subject of the passage?
- What point is the author making about this subject?

Preview:

Write a brief summary of the passage you just read.

Summary:

Choose the *best* answer for each of the following questions.

1. In the first sentence of the passage, the author's use of "we" means

    a. everyone;
    b. people who live on farms;
    c. scholars;
    d. those who live in the past.

2. The author implies that people

    a. are at the mercy of fate;
    b. believe they have more freedom than they really do;
    c. have less freedom now than a generation before them;
    d. have some control over their lives.

3. Thoreau admires the cock because it apparently recognizes that

    a. nature continues unchanged;
    b. change is constant;
    c. it lives outside of civilization;
    d. it is so beautiful.

4. "Fugitive slave laws," in the author's view, are enforced by those who

    a. address a future problem;
    b. try to keep the past alive;
    c. concentrate on current problems;
    d. prefer to live in the past.

5. The author's attitude toward the subject is

    a. uncompromising;
    b. vacillating;
    c. ambiguous;
    d. indifferent.

From "England in 1685," Thomas Macaulay

Prompt: Recall a place that has been improved.

The market place which the rustic can now reach with his cart in an hour was, a hundred and sixty years ago, a day's journey from him. The street which now affords to the artisan, during the whole night, a secure, a convenient, and a brilliantly lighted walk was, a hundred and sixty years ago, so dark after sunset that he would not have been able to see his hand, so ill-paved that he would have run constant risk of breaking his neck, and so ill-watched that he would have been in imminent danger of being knocked down and plundered of his small earnings. Every bricklayer who falls from a scaffold, every sweeper of a crossing who is run over by a carriage, may now have his wounds dressed and his limbs set with a skill such as, a hundred and sixty years ago, all the wealth of a great lord like Ormond, or of a merchant prince like Clayton, could not have purchased. Some frightful diseases have been extirpated by science; and some have been banished by police. The term of human life has been lengthened over the whole kingdom, and especially in the towns. The year 1685 was not accounted sickly; yet in the year 1685 more than one in twenty-three of the inhabitants of the capital died. At present only one inhabitant in forty dies annually. The difference in salubrity between the London of the nineteenth century and the London of the seventeenth century is very far greater than the difference between London in an ordinary season and London in the cholera.

Still more important is the benefit which all orders of society, and especially the lower orders, have derived from the mollifying influence of civilization on the national character. The groundwork of that character has indeed been the same through many generations, in the sense in which the groundwork of the character of an individual may be said to be the same when he is a rude and thoughtless schoolboy and when he is a refined and accomplished man. It is pleasing to reflect that the public mind of England has softened while it has ripened, and that we have, in the course of ages, become, not only a wiser, but also a kinder people. There is scarcely a page of the history or lighter literature of the seventeenth century which does not contain some proof that our ancestors were less humane than their posterity. The discipline of workshops, of schools, of private families, though not more efficient than at present, was infinitely harsher. Masters, well born and bred, were in the habit of beating their servants. Pedagogues knew no way of imparting knowledge but by beating their pupils. Husbands, of decent station, were not ashamed to beat their wives. The implacability of hostile factions was such as we can scarcely conceive.

Preview the passage to gain an overview. Then write your answers to the following questions:

- What is the subject of the passage?
- What point is the author making about this subject?

Preview:

Write a brief summary of the passage you just read.

Summary:

Choose the *best* answer for each of the following questions:

1. The author compares

   a. the city and the country;
   b. England and France;
   c. England of the 17th century and England of the 19th century;
   d. capitalism and socialism.

2. According to the author, life has improved in all areas *except*

   a. medical care;
   b. conditions in the market;
   c. religious life;
   d. life span.

3. The meaning of "extirpated" (line 15) could be

    a. exaggerated;
    b. eliminated;
    c. machine made;
    d. misunderstood.

4. In making his point the author refers to all *except*

    a. statistics;
    b. details;
    c. names of individuals;
    d. sociological studies.

5. The tone of this piece is

    a. positive;
    b. pessimistic;
    c. ambiguous;
    d. threatening.

From *The Prince,* Niccolo Machiavelli

Prompt: Would you rather be loved or feared?

Here a question arises: Whether it is better to be loved than feared, or the reverse. The answer is, of course, that it would be best to be both loved and feared. But since the two rarely come together, anyone compelled to choose will find greater security in being feared than in being loved. For this can be said about the generality of men: that they are ungrateful, fickle, dissembling, anxious to flee danger, and covetous of gain. So long as you promote their advantage, they are all yours, as I said before, and will offer you their blood, their goods, their lives, and their children when the need for these is remote. When the need arises, however, they will turn against you. The prince who bases his security upon their word, lacking other provision is doomed; for friendships that are gained by money, not by greatness and nobility of spirit, may well be earned, but cannot be kept; and in the time of need, they will have fled your purse. Men are less concerned about offending someone they have cause to love than someone they have cause to fear. Love endures by a bond which men, being scoundrels, may break whenever it serves their advantage to do so; but fear is supported by the dread of pain, which is ever present.

Preview the passage to gain an overview. Then write your answers to the following questions:

- What is the subject of the passage?
- What point is the author making about this subject?

Preview:

Write a brief summary of the passage you just read.

Summary:

Choose the *best* answer for each of the following questions.

1. According to the author, is it better to be feared or loved, and why?

    a. It is better to be loved because kindness produces loyalty.
    b. It is better to be feared because history has shown that the greatest rulers capitalized on people's fears.
    c. It is better to be feared because fear produces loyalty.
    d. It is better to be loved because people respect those they love more than those they fear.
    e. It is better to be feared because men like to offend those they fear.

2. What does this passage assume about human nature?

    a. The passage assumes people are basically good at heart.
    b. This passage acknowledges that people are usually seeking pleasure and avoiding pain.
    c. Human nature is easy to understand and manipulate.
    d. Human nature is most often unselfish and steady.
    e. b and c

3. What evidence does the author cite to prove his point?

    a. The author cites no evidence.
    b. The author cites his own experience to prove the point.
    c. The author cites primary sources from history.
    d. The author cites scholarly critical analysis to bolster his argument.
    e. The author cites well-known examples from psychological studies.

4. What do people value most, according to this passage?

    a. wealth;
    b. respect;
    c. love;
    d. family;
    e. friendship.

5. To whom is this advice directed?

    a.   to anyone who needs it;
    b.   to leaders and rulers;
    c.   to members of royalty;
    d.   to someone involved in a troubled relationship;
    e.   to members of the working class.

From *On Liberty,* John Stuart Mill

Prompt: How many kinds of liberty can you think of?

The object of this essay is to assert one very simple principle, as entitled to govern absolutely the dealings of society with the individual in the way of compulsion and control, whether the means used be physical force in the form of legal penalties or the moral coercion of public opinion. That principle is that the sole end for which mankind are warranted, individually or collectively, in interfering with the liberty of action of any of their number is self-protection. That the only purpose for which power can be rightfully exercised over any member of a civilized community, against his will, is to prevent harm to others. His own good, either physical or moral, is not a sufficient warrant. He cannot rightfully be compelled to do or forbear because it will be better for him to do so, because it will make him happier, because, in the opinions of others, to do so would be wise or even right. These are good reasons for remonstrating with him, or reasoning with him, or persuading him, or entreating him or visiting him with any evil in case he do otherwise. To justify that, the conduct from which it is desired to deter him must be calculated to produce evil to someone else. The only part of the conduct of anyone for which he is amenable to society is that which concerns himself, his independence is, of right, absolute. Over himself, over his own body and mind, the individual is sovereign.

Preview the passage to gain an overview. Then write your answers to the following questions:

- What is the subject of the passage?
- What point is the author making about this subject?

Preview:

Write a brief summary of the passage you just read.

Summary:

Choose the *best* answer for each of the following questions.

1. According to the author, who or what is responsible for an individual's thoughts and physical well-being?

    a. society;
    b. parents;
    c. the individual;
    d. schools;
    e. government.

2. What does the passage refer to as "moral coercion"?

    a. public opinion;
    b. the law;
    c. psychological principles;
    d. the social contract;
    e. none of the above.

3. What does the author state is the "only purpose for which power can be rightfully exercised over any member of a civilized community, against his will"?

    a. to prevent harm to himself or herself;
    b. for the good of society;
    c. when it is morally right;
    d. for a good and just cause;
    e. to prevent harm to others.

4. What does the author offer as an alternative to exercising power over another?

    a. reasoning with him;
    b. persuading him;
    c. compelling him;
    d. threatening him;
    e. a and b.

From the "Cross of Gold" Speech, William Jennings Bryan

Prompt: Why should we have an income tax?

We do not come as aggressors. Our war is not a war of conquest; we are fighting in the defense of our homes, our families, and posterity. We have petitioned, and our petitions have been scorned. We have entreated, and our entreaties have been disregarded. We have begged, and they have mocked when our calamity came. We beg no longer; we entreat no more; we petition no more. We defy them!

The gentleman from Wisconsin has said that he fears a Robespierre. My friends, in this land of the free you need not fear that a tyrant will spring up from among the people. What we need is an Andrew Jackson to stand, as Jackson stood, against the encroachments of organized wealth.

They tell us that this platform was made to catch votes. We reply to them that changing conditions make new issues; that the principles upon which Democracy rests are as everlasting as the hills, but that they must be applied to new conditions as they arise. Conditions have arisen, and we are here to meet those conditions. They tell us that the income tax ought not to be brought in here; that it is a new idea. They criticize us for our criticism of the Supreme Court of the United States. My friends, we have not criticized, we have simply called attention to what you already know. If you want criticisms, read the dissenting opinions of the court. There you will find criticisms. They say that we passed an unconstitutional law; we deny it. The income tax was not unconstitutional when it went before the Supreme Court for the first time; it did not become unconstitutional until one of the judges changed his mind, and we cannot be expected to know when a judge will change his mind. The income tax is just. It simply intends to put the burdens of government justly upon the backs of the people. I am in favor of an income tax. When I find a man who is not willing to bear his share of the burdens of the government which protects him, I find a man who is unworthy to enjoy the blessings of a government like ours.

Preview the passage to gain an overview. Then write your answers to the following questions:

- What is the subject of the passage?
- What point is the author making about this subject?

Preview:

Write a brief summary of the passage you just read.

Summary:

Choose the *best* answer for each of the following questions.

1. What is the speaker's perspective about an income tax?

    a. He is in favor of it if only the upper class is taxed.
    b. He is in favor of it if only the lower class is taxed.
    c. He will be in favor of it if his audience decides in favor of it.
    d. He is in favor of it.
    e. He is not in favor of it.

2. From your reading of this passage, what was the Supreme Court's decision on the constitutional nature of the income tax?

    a. It reaffirmed the constitutionality of the law passed by the legislature.
    b. It ruled that the legislature passed an unconstitutional law.
    c. It ruled that the legislature is allowed to pass what it sees fit.
    d. It ruled that only income tax, and no other form of taxation, is constitutional.
    e. This passage gives no account of the Supreme Court's decision.

3. Who is the speaker addressing, as evidenced by his choice of words and tone of voice?

    a. Congress;
    b. the Supreme Court;
    c. the Democratic convention;
    d. cannot be inferred from this passage;
    e. the general public.

4. According to this excerpt, why does the speaker feel that the income tax is just?

    a. because the people should bear the burdens of government;
    b. because government should bear its own burdens;
    c. because any form of taxation is just as long as it serves the people;
    d. because the speaker feels that some individuals must never reach an income that exceeds another's income;
    e. because taxation would affect all citizens equally.

From *The Peloponnesian War,* Thucydides

Prompt: Why do nations go to war?

If you give way, you will instantly have to meet some greater demand, as having been frightened into obedience in the first instance; but a firm refusal will make them clearly understand that they must treat you more as equals. Make your decision therefore at once, either to submit before you are harmed, or if we are to go to war, as I for one think we ought, to do so without caring whether the ostensible cause be great or small, resolved against making concessions or consenting to a precarious tenure of our possessions. For all claims from an equal, urged upon a neighbor as commands, before any attempt at legal settlement, be they great or be they small, have only one meaning, and that is slavery.

As to the war and the resources of either party, a detailed comparison will not show you the inferiority of Athens. Personally engaged in the cultivation of their land, without funds either private or public, the Peloponnesians are also without experience in long wars across sea, from the strict limit which poverty imposes on their attacks upon each other. Powers of this description are quite incapable of often manning a fleet or often sending out an army; they cannot afford the absence from their homes, and the expenditure from their own funds; and besides, they have not command of the sea. Capital, it must be remembered, maintains a war more than forced contributions.

Preview the passage to gain an overview. Then write your answers to the following questions:

- What is the subject of the passage?
- What point is the author making about this subject?

Preview:

Write a brief summary of the passage you just read.

Summary:

Choose the *best* answer for each of the following questions.

1. What is the speaker trying to persuade his audience to do?

   a. to go to war after more debate and deliberation;
   b. to go to war immediately;
   c. to avoid war at all costs;
   d. to avoid war if the neighboring country refuses;
   e. to carry out a surprise attack on the neighboring country.

2. To what does the speaker equate acquiescing to his neighbor's commands?

   a. wisdom;
   b. resignation;
   c. choice;
   d. slavery;
   e. blasphemy.

3. Which is *not* one of the stated reasons why the neighboring country would lose?

   a. The neighboring country is mostly populated with farmers.
   b. The farming population has little capital with which to fund a war.
   c. The neighbors have no experience in wars of the kind which would be fought.
   d. The neighbors do not have enough men or funds for an army or a naval fleet.
   e. The neighbors have little military skill and fewer available weapons.

4. What would happen, he warns, if an appeasement
    policy is implemented?

    a. Their country would have to meet more and greater
        demands.
    b. The conflict could be diffused.
    c. The neighboring country would treat them more as
        equals.
    d. Their country would be at an advantage if tensions
        increased.
    e. The neighboring country would be at a military dis-
        advantage.

From "Wealth against Commonwealth," Henry Demarest Lloyd

Prompt: Who deserves to be wealthy?

Nature is rich; but everywhere man, the heir of nature, is poor. Never in this happy country or elsewhere—except in the Land of Miracle, where 'they did all eat and were filled'—has there been enough of anything for the people. Never since time began have all the sons and daughters of men been all warm, and all filled, and all shod and roofed. Never yet have all the virgins, wise or foolish, been able to fill their lamps with oil.

The world, enriched by thousands of generations of toilers and thinkers, has reached a fertility which can give every human being a plenty undreamed of even in the Utopias. But between this plenty ripening on the boughs of our civilization and the people hungering for it step the 'corners,' the syndicates, trusts, combinations, with the cry of 'over-production'—too much of everything. Holding back the riches of earth, sea, and sky from their fellows who famish and freeze in the dark, they declare to them that there is too much light and warmth and food. They assert the right, for their private profit, to regulate the consumption by the people of the necessaries of life, and to control production, not by the needs of humanity, but by the desires of a few for dividends. The coal syndicate thinks there is too much coal. There is too much iron, too much lumber, too much flour—for this or that syndicate.

The majority have never been able to buy enough of anything; but this minority have too much of everything to sell.

Liberty produces wealth and wealth destroys liberty.

Preview the passage to gain an overview. Then write your answers to the following questions:

- What is the subject of the passage?
- What point is the author making about this subject?

Preview:

Write a brief summary of the passage you just read.

Summary:

Choose the *best* answer for each of the following questions.

1. What is the object of the speaker's wrath?

    a. monopolies and big business;
    b. communists;
    c. affluent men and women;
    d. lawyers;
    e. government officials.

2. What, according to the speaker, is the original state of
    nature?

    a. harsh and cold;
    b. rough, but made easier by human accomplishment;
    c. abundance for the elite few;
    d. abundance for those who are willing to work;
    e. rich, fertile, and plentiful for all.

3. What is *not* standing between people and nature's plenty?

    a. syndicates;
    b. trusts;
    c. combinations;
    d. government;
    e. a, b, and c

4. By inferring from this passage, can you tell how wealth
    destroys liberty?

    a. by putting power to control life's necessities in
        the hands of an uneducated majority;
    b. by putting all the power to control life's necessities
        in the hands of a minority;
    c. by allowing people too much freedom and thereby
        enslaving them;
    d. the passage does not state that wealth destroys
        liberty;
    e. by allowing too much wealth to interfere with
        what's really important.

From "True End of Civil Government," John Locke

Prompt: Where should the government get its power?

The power that every individual gave the society when he entered into it, can never revert to the individuals again, as long as the society lasts, but will always remain in the community; because without this there can be no community, no commonwealth, which is contrary to the original agreement; so also when the society hath placed the legislative in any assembly of men, to continue in them and their successors, with direction and authority for providing such successors, the legislative can never revert to the people whilst that government lasts; because having provided a legislative with power to continue for ever, they have given up their political power to the legislative, and cannot resume it. But if they have set limits to the duration of their legislative, and made this supreme power in any person or assembly only temporary; or else when, by the miscarriages of those in authority, it is forfeited; upon the forfeiture of their rulers, or at the determination of the time set, it reverts to the society, and the people have a right to act as supreme, and continue the legislative in themselves or place it in a new form, or new hands, as they think good.

Preview the passage to gain an overview. Then write your answers to the following questions:

- What is the subject of the passage?
- What point is the author making about this subject?

Preview:

Write a brief summary of the passage you just read.

Summary:

Choose the *best* answer for each of the following questions.

1. According to this passage, who in society most often holds the political power?

    a. the legislative;
    b. the general public;
    c. the judiciary;
    d. all members of society are equal in terms of political power;
    e. the supreme ruler.

2. Without the _____ given society by each individual, there can be no community.

    a. capital;
    b. choice;
    c. power;
    d. understanding;
    e. freedom.

3. What consequence does the author envision once an assembly has been established?

    a. Legislative control can never go back to the people while that government exists.
    b. The legislative power can return to the people's hands at any time.
    c. The legislative can go back to the people if they reaffirm the power of the existing government.
    d. The people never relinquish control of the legislative.
    e. The people are not allowed control of the legislative under any circumstances.

4. In this author's view, the people may act as supreme if

    a. they had set limits to the duration of the legislative;
    b. the legislative power was forfeited by a miscarriage of authority;
    c. a and b;
    d. they vote;
    e. the people can never act as supreme.

From "The American Crisis," Thomas Paine, and "The Controversy between Great Britain and Her Colonies," Samuel Seabury

Prompt: Would you have supported the American Revolution?

From "The American Crisis" (Paine)

These are the times that try men's souls. The summer soldier and the sunshine patriot will, in this crisis, shrink from the service of his country; but he that stands it NOW, deserves the love and thanks of man and woman. Tyranny, like hell, is not easily conquered; yet we have this consolation with us, that the harder the conflict, the more glorious the triumph. What we obtain too cheap, we esteem too lightly: "tis dearness only that gives every thing its value." Heaven knows how to put a proper price upon its goods; and it would be strange indeed, if so celestial an article as FREEDOM should not be highly rated. Britain, with an army to enforce her tyranny, has declared that she has a right (*not only* to TAX) but "to BIND *us* in ALL CASES WHATSOEVER," and if being *bound in that manner,* is not slavery, then is there not such a thing as slavery upon earth. Even the expression is impious, for so unlimited a power can belong only to God.

Whether the independence of the continent was declared too soon or delayed too long, I will not now enter into an argument; my own simple opinion is, that had it been eight months earlier, it would have been much better. We did not make a proper use of last winter, neither could we, while we were in a dependent state. However, the fault, if it were one, was all our own; we have none to blame but ourselves. But no great deal is lost yet; all that Howe has been doing for this month past, is rather a ravage than a conquest, which the spirit of the Jerseys a year ago would have quickly repulsed, and which time and a little resolution will soon recover.

I have as little superstition in me as any man living, but my secret opinion has ever been, and still is, that God Almighty will not give up a people to military destruction, or leave them unsupportedly to perish, who have so earnestly and so repeatedly sought to avoid the calamities of war, by every decent method which wisdom could invent. Neither have I so much of the infidel in me, as to suppose that He has relinquished the government of the world, and given us up to the care of devils;

and as I do not, I cannot see on what grounds the king of Britain can look up to Heaven for help against us: a common murderer, a highwayman, or a housebreaker, has as good a pretence as he.

From "The Controversy Between Great Britain and Her Colonies" (Seabury)

I wish you had explicitly declared to the public your ideas of the natural rights of mankind. Man in a state of nature may be considered as perfectly free from all restraints of law and government; and then the weak must submit to the strong. From such a state, I confess, I have a violent aversion. I think the form of government we lately enjoyed provides a much more eligible state to live in, and cannot help regretting our having lost it by the equity, wisdom, and authority of the Congress, who have introduced in the room of it confusion and violence, where all must submit to the power of a mob.

You have taken some pains to prove what would readily have been granted you—that liberty is a very good thing, and slavery a very bad thing. But then I must think that liberty under a king, Lords, and Commons is as good as liberty under a republican Congress; and that slavery under a republican Congress is as bad, at least, as slavery under a king, Lords, and Commons; and, upon the whole, that liberty under the supreme authority and protection of Great Britain is infinitely preferable to slavery under an American Congress. I will also agree with you "that Americans are entitled to freedom." I will go further: I will own and acknowledge that not only Americans but Africans, Europeans, Asiatics, all men of all countries and degrees, of all sizes and complexions, have a right to as much freedom as is consistent with the security of civil society. And I hope you will not think me an "enemy" to the natural "rights of mankind" because I cannot wish them more. We must, however, remember that more liberty may, without inconvenience, be allowed to individuals in a small government than can be admitted of in a large empire.

But when you assert that "since Americans have not by any act of theirs empowered the British Parliament to make laws for them, it follows they can have no just authority to do it," you advance a position subversive of that dependence which all colonies must, from their very nature, have on the mother country. By the British Parliament, I suppose you mean the supreme legislative authority, the King, Lords, and Commons, because no other authority in England has a right to make laws to bind the kingdom, and consequently no authority to make laws to bind the colonies. In this sense I shall understand and use the phrase "British Parliament."

Now the dependence of the colonies on the mother country has ever been acknowledged. It is an impropriety of speech to talk of an independent colony. The words "independency" and "colony" convey contradictory ideas: much like killing and sparing. As soon as a colony becomes independent of its parent state, it ceases to be any longer a colony; just as when you kill a sheep, you cease to spare him. The British colonies make a part of the British Empire. As parts of the body they must be subject to the general laws of the body. To talk of a colony independent of the mother country is no better sense than to talk of a limb independent of the body to which it belongs.

Preview each passage to gain an overview. Then write your answers to the following questions:

- What is the subject of each passage?
- What point is the author making about this subject?

Previews:

Write a brief summary of each of the passages you just read.

Summaries:

Choose the *best* answer for each of the following questions.

1. In the first two sentences, Paine distinguishes between
   a. the old and the young;
   b. the religious and the irreligious;
   c. the loyal and the disloyal;
   d. British and Americans.

2. Paine criticizes the British primarily because he
    believes

    a. they have denied the colonists' religious freedom;
    b. they have assumed God's power;
    c. they have overpriced tea;
    d. they have debased the colonists' values.

3. In Paine's view, if the colonists had declared war
    earlier, they would have

    a. gained a psychological advantage;
    b. become much better organized;
    c. lost some key battles;
    d. held back some British advances.

4. Paine views the struggle for independence, above all, as

    a. a moral issue;
    b. an economic issue;
    c. a political issue;
    d. a psychological issue.

5. In the passage, Paine uses

    a. statistics;
    b. figures of speech;
    c. shifts in points of view;
    d. acronyms.

6. Seabury fears the power of the

    a. king;
    b. mob;
    c. British government;
    d. nature.

7. The person to whom Seabury responds apparently be-
    lieves that the British

    a. have no legitimate authority over the colonists;
    b. should join the colonists in a new government;
    c. should abandon their government;
    d. should continue to have authority over the colonies.

8. Seabury would not grant any liberties that caused the

    a. closing of Parliament;
    b. slaves to be freed;
    c. breakdown of civil society;
    d. people to return to a state of nature.

9. Seabury claims it is impossible to consider colonists as

    a. British subjects;
    b. anything but slaves;
    c. capable of running a government;
    d. independent individuals.

10. Seabury compares the colonists to

    a. stones on the beach;
    b. stars in the sky;
    c. limbs of a body;
    d. articles of clothing in a wardrobe.

11. Seabury and Paine have different views on

    a. the ultimate source of authority;
    b. the cause of wars;
    c. the most effective form of democratic government;
    d. the role of women.

12. Paine, more than Seabury, seems to believe in the basic goodness of

    a. human nature;
    b. the American constitution;
    c. colonial leaders;
    d. colonial religious leaders.

13. Paine and Seabury disagree on all of the issues *except*

    a. the ultimate source of authority;
    b. human nature;
    c. the obligation of the colonists;
    d. the desirability of individual liberty.

Readings in Science

SOME GUIDELINES

The readings in this section have scientific topics. Several of the readings discuss evolution, natural selection, and the effect of heredity upon survival. The balance address a variety of topics, including population growth, the functioning of the human mind, and the process of scientific investigation.

Readings on scientific subjects such as these are frequently included on achievement tests. The current practice, in fact, is to include several readings on a single given topic. As with previous readings, determine the central point, note supporting examples, and study carefully the questions listed at the end of each reading passage. In doing so you will be reading actively, which is essential to reading well.

Remember to practice the three steps to strategic reading:

1. Preview before you read.
2. Underline and annotate while you read.
3. Summarize after you read.

From "Mechanic Arts," Samuel Miller

Prompt: Why are we living better now?

Finally, the effects of the various improvements which have been introduced into every department of the mechanic arts, during the last age, in promoting the conveniency, cheapness, and elegance of *living,* will readily occur to the most careless observer. No one will say that it indicates undue partiality to our own times to assert, that at no period of the world was the *art of living,* especially the comforts and conveniences of domestic life, ever on so advantageous a footing as at present. Ancient writers, indeed have given highly coloured pictures of the magnificence and sensuality which reigned at different times, in *Greece* and *Rome;* and in more modern days we read many descriptions of luxury which superficial thinkers would suppose to indicate much greater plenty, comfort, and splendour, than are now commonly enjoyed. But they are, for the most part, descriptions of plenty without taste; and of luxury without enjoyment. When we compare the ancient modes of living with the dress, the furniture, the equipage, the conveniences of travelling, and the incomparably greater ease with which the same amount of comfortable accommodation may be obtained at present, none can hesitate to give a decided preference, in all these respects, to modern times. Perhaps it would not be extravagant to say that many of the higher orders of mechanics and day labourers now wear better clothes, and live not more plentifully, but in some respects more conveniently, more neatly, and with more true taste, than many princes and kings were in the habit of doing two centuries ago, and in a manner quite as pleasant as multitudes of a rank far superior to themselves, at a later period. In short, the remarkable and unprecedented union of neatness and simplicity, cheapness and elegance, which has been exhibited, in the art of living, within the last thirty or forty years, is, at once, a testimony of the rapid improvement of the mechanic arts, and one of the most unquestionable points in which we may claim a superiority over our predecessors.

Preview the passage to gain an overview. Then write your answers to the following questions:

- What is the subject of the passage?
- What point is the author making about this subject?

Preview:

Write a brief summary of the passage you just read.

Summary:

Choose the *best* answer for each of the following questions.

1. Does the author feel that the present standard of living is superior or inferior to past civilizations?

   a. He implies that our present standard of living is deficient in terms of the mechanical gains we have made.
   b. He feels that the present standard of living far exceeds that of past centuries.
   c. He feels that Greco-Roman culture is the only ancient civilization to which ours can be compared.
   d. He states that the present standard of living falls short of past centuries only slightly, a condition attributed to the modern emphasis on culture over science.
   e. He fails to state an opinion on the present standard of living.

2. What, in the author's terms, brought about a higher standard of living?

   a. the mechanic arts;
   b. an improvement in human intellectual capacity;
   c. a statistically significant increase in the amount of conveniences being manufactured;
   d. a decline in the apprenticeship tradition of labour;
   e. interchangeable parts.

3. In what time period was this passage written?

   a. 1700–1800;
   b. 1800–1850;
   c. 1850–1900;
   d. 1900–present;
   e. impossible to infer from the information given.

4. What exactly are the "mechanic arts"?

   a. literary advances that produce a union of neatness and simplicity, cheapness and elegance exhibited in everyday life;
   b. sculpture and painting that exhibit the inner workings of technological advances;
   c. technological advances that produce a union of neatness and simplicity, cheapness and elegance exhibited in everyday life;
   d. new modes of mechanics that can be utilized by every person in society, regardless of economic background or technical skill;
   e. technological advances that will be used by experts to overcome present obstacles to scientific breakthroughs.

From *On the Origin of Species,* Charles Darwin

Prompt: What have you learned about evolution?

Natural selection acts solely through the preservation of variations in some way advantageous, which consequently endure. But as from the high geometrical powers of increase of all organic beings, each area is already fully stocked with inhabitants, it follows that as each selected and favoured form increases in number, so will the less favoured forms decrease and become rare. Rarity, as geology tells us, is the precursor to extinction. We can, also, see that any form represented by few individuals will, during fluctuations in the seasons or in the number of its enemies, run a good chance of utter extinction. But we may go further than this; for as new forms are continually and slowly being produced, unless we believe that the number of specific forms goes on perpetually and almost indefinitely increasing, numbers inevitably must become extinct. That the number of specific forms has not indefinitely increased, geology shows us plainly; and indeed we can see reason why they should not have thus increased, for the number of places in the polity of nature is not indefinitely great—not that we have any means of knowing that any one region has as yet got its maximum of species.

Preview the passage to gain an overview. Then write your answers to the following questions:

- What is the subject of the passage?
- What point is the author making about this subject?

Preview:

Write a brief summary of the passage you just read.

Summary:

Choose the *best* answer for each of the following questions.

1. In this passage, what inevitably and initially occurs for less-favored life forms?

   a. They become more and more rare.
   b. They become more fruitful.
   c. They become more diverse.
   d. They become rare at first and then multiply as a result of their dormancy.
   e. b and c

2. The author specifically states that rarity is the precursor to

   a. profusion
   b. availability
   c. purity
   d. enrichment
   e. extinction

3. As noted in the passage, what does geology reveal?

   a. The number of specific forms has indefinitely increased.
   b. The number of specific forms has not indefinitely increased.
   c. The kinds of forms have become more and more beautiful.
   d. Different kinds of forms have become harder and harder to locate.
   e. The passage fails to mention geology.

4. What can cause the ultimate extinction of the few rare individuals to which the author alludes?

   a. fluctuations in the seasons;
   b. fluctuations in the number of its enemies;
   c. a and b;
   d. the innate ability to extinguish their own lives;
   e. none of the above.

From *On the Origin of Species,* Charles Darwin

Prompt: Are you equipped to survive?

Can the principle of selection, which we have seen is so potent in the hands of man, apply in nature? I think we shall see that it can act most effectually. Let it be borne in mind in what an endless number of strange peculiarities our domestic productions, and, in a lesser degree, those under nature vary; and how strong the hereditary tendency is. Under domestication, it may be truly said that the whole organization becomes in some degree plastic. Let it be borne in mind how infinitely complex and close-fitting are the mutual relations of all organic beings to each other and to their physical conditions of life. Can it, then, be thought improbable, seeing that variations useful to man have undoubtedly occurred, that other variations useful in some way to each being in the great and complex battle of life, should sometimes occur in the course of thousands of generations?

If such do occur, can we doubt (remembering that many more individuals are born than can possibly survive) that individuals having any advantage, however slight, over others, would have the best chance of surviving and of procreating their kind? On the other hand, we may feel sure that any variation in the least degree injurious would be rigidly destroyed. This preservation of favourable variations, I call Natural Selection. Variations neither useful nor injurious would not be affected by natural selection, and would be left a fluctuating element as perhaps we see in the species called polymorphic.

Preview the passage to gain an overview. Then write your answers to the following questions:

- What is the subject of the passage?
- What point is the author making about this subject?

Preview:

Write a brief summary of the passage you just read.

Summary:

Choose the *best* answer to each of the following questions.

1. What does the author mean by the term "plastic"?

   a. artificial;
   b. malleable;
   c. hard;
   d. mass-produced;
   e. clear.

2. On what premise does the author base his conclusions?

   a. There is great variation in the wide number of existing organisms which can be strongly traced through heredity.
   b. All organisms are exactly the same in their original physical state.
   c. Some humans are intrinsically better than others.
   d. Humans and animals must have a few differences, but these do not matter in light of their biological similarities.
   e. Natural selection has been decreed by a higher power.

3. As indicated by the author, what kind of individuals survive best?

   a. those with a physical disadvantage;
   b. those with a physical disadvantage and mental superiority;
   c. those with any sort of physical advantage useful to humankind;
   d. those with a physical advantage and mental inferiority;
   e. those with a kind nature and brute strength.

4. Why does the author term this process a "natural" selection?

    a. The organisms themselves unconsciously implement this process.
    b. It is done in accordance with the necessity of nature, regardless of human conscious thought.
    c. It feels right to the organisms involved.
    d. The process should not be countered by rational thought.
    e. To select some organisms for survival over others is inherent in human nature.

From *On the Origin of Species,* Charles Darwin

Prompt: How does the mind of a higher animal compare to a human mind?

There can be no doubt that the difference between the mind of the lowest man and that of the highest animal is immense. An anthropomorphous ape, if he could take a dispassionate view of his own case, would admit that though he could form an artful plan to plunder a garden—though he could use stones for fighting or for breaking open nuts, yet that the thought of fashioning a stone into a tool was quite beyond his scope. Still less, as he would admit, could he follow out a train of metaphysical reasoning, or solve a mathematical problem, or reflect on God, or admire a grand natural scene. Some apes, however, would probably declare that they could and did admire the beauty of the coloured skin and fur of their partners in marriage. They would admit, that though they could make other apes understand by cries some of their perceptions and simpler wants, the notion of expressing definite ideas by definite sounds had never crossed their minds. They might insist that they were ready to aid their fellow-apes of the same troop in many ways, to risk their lives for them, and to take charge of their orphans; but they would be forced to acknowledge that disinterested love for all living creatures, the most noble attribute of man, was quite beyond their comprehension.

Nevertheless the difference in minds between man and the higher animals, great as it is, certainly is one of degree and not of kind. We have seen that the senses and intuitions, the various emotions and faculties, such as love, memory, attention, curiosity, imitation, reason, etc., of which man boasts, may be found in an incipient, or even sometimes in a well-developed condition, in the lower animals. They are also capable of some inherited improvement, as we see in the domestic dog compared with the wolf or jackal. If it could be proved that certain high mental powers, such as the formation of general concepts, self-consciousness, etc., were absolutely peculiar to man, which seems extremely doubtful, it is not improbable that these qualities are merely the incidental results of other highly advanced intellectual faculties; and these again mainly the result of the continued use of a perfect language. At what age does the new-born infant possess the power of abstraction, or become self-conscious, and reflect on its own existence? We cannot answer; nor can we answer in regard to the ascending organic scale. The half-art, half-instinct of language still bears the stamp of its gradual evolution. The ennobling belief in God is not universal with man; and the belief in spiritual agencies naturally follows from other mental powers. The moral sense perhaps affords the best and highest distinction between man and the lower animals; but I need say nothing on this head, as I have so lately endeavoured to shew that the social instincts—the prime principle of man's moral constitution—with the aid of active intellectual powers and the effects of habit, naturally lead to the golden rule, "As ye would that men should do to you, do ye to them likewise"; and this lies at the foundation of morality.

Preview the passage to gain an overview. Then write your answers to the following questions:

- What is the subject of the passage?
- What point is the author making about this subject?

Preview:

Write a brief summary of the passage you just read.

Summary:

Choose the *best* answer to each of the following questions.

1. The meaning of "anthropomorphous" could be

   a. threatening;
   b. humanlike;
   c. primitive;
   d. evolutionary.

2. The author

   a. uses extended metaphors;
   b. imagines the thoughts of another being;
   c. refers to studies;
   d. speaks in the second person.

3. According to the author, certain animals can

   a. reflect on God;
   b. use weapons;
   c. use tools;
   d. make weapons and tools.

4. The most noble of man's attributes, according to the author, is

   a. desire to love;
   b. ability to form societies;
   c. unbiased affection for all living things;
   d. self consciousness.

5. The author is uncertain of all the following *except*

   a. the degree to which animals experience emotions;
   b. how much animals can improve through heredity;
   c. when infants develop the ability of abstraction;
   d. that the golden rule is the foundation of morality.

From *Evolution and Ethics,* T. H. Huxley

Prompt: What do the words "cosmic process" mean to you?

Men in society are undoubtedly subject to the cosmic process. As among other animals, multiplication goes on without cessation, and involves severe competition for the means of support. The struggle for existence tends to eliminate those less fitted to adapt themselves to the circumstances of their existence. The strongest, the most self-assertive, tend to tread down the weaker. But the influence of the cosmic process on the evolution of society is the greater the more rudimentary its civilization. Social progress means a checking of the cosmic process at every step and the substitution for it of another, which may be called the ethical process; the end of which is not the survival of those who may happen to be the fittest, in respect of the whole of the conditions which obtain, but of those who are ethically the best.

As I have already urged, the practice of that which is ethically best—what we call goodness or virtue—involves a course of conduct which, in all respects, is opposed to that which leads to success in the cosmic struggle for existence. In place of ruthless self-assertion it demands self-restraint; in place of thrusting aside, or treading down, all competitors, it requires that the individual shall not merely respect, but shall help his fellows; its influence is directed, not so much to the survival of the fittest, as to the fitting of as many as possible to survive. It repudiates the gladiatorial theory of existence. It demands that each man who enters into the enjoyment of the advantages of a polity shall be mindful of his debt to those who have laboriously constructed it; and shall take heed that no act of his weakens the fabric in which he has been permitted to live. Laws and moral precepts are directed to the end of curbing the cosmic process and reminding the individual of his duty to the community, to the protection and influence of which he owes, if not existence itself, at least the life of something better than a brutal savage.

Preview the passage to gain an overview. Then write your answers to the following questions:

- What is the subject of the passage?
- What point is the author making about this subject?

Preview:

Write a brief summary of the passage you just read.

Summary:

Choose the *best* answer to each of the following questions.

1. What is the "cosmic process" to which the author refers?

    a. evolution;
    b. astronomical activity;
    c. astrological activity;
    d. the life cycle;
    e. scientific discovery.

2. What does the author recommend humankind should do to check the cosmic process?

    a. remain neutral in dealing with other individuals;
    b. display ruthless self-assertion;
    c. show goodness and virtue by helping other individuals;
    d. offer help only to deserving individuals;
    e. follow strict guidelines set forth by the scientific community.

3. What examples does the passage detail which support curbing the cosmic process?

    a. laws;
    b. moral precepts;
    c. brute force;
    d. philosophy;
    e. a and b.

4. What effect does the author see this kind of check having on the social order?

    a.   Society and community would be strengthened as each individual owes allegiance to the community above his or her self.

    b.   The sense of community would be weakened as people fight to help others and lose sight of themselves.

    c.   The social order will dissolve into chaos as people ignore the laws and precepts that refute human nature.

    d.   The social order is unified as people are allowed to follow their true natures.

    e.   The sense of community remains exactly the same as people continue acting like brutal savages.

From *On the Relations of Man to the Lower Animals,* T. H. Huxley

Prompt: Are people basically selfish?

Or is the philanthropist or the saint to give up his endeavors to lead a noble life, because the simplest study of man's nature reveals, at its foundations, all the selfish passions and fierce appetites of the merest quadruped? Is mother-love vile because a hen shows it, or fidelity base because dogs possess it?

The common sense of the mass of mankind will answer these questions without a moment's hesitation. Healthy humanity, finding itself hard pressed to escape from real sin and degradation, will leave the brooding over speculative pollution to the cynics and the "righteous overmuch" who, disagreeing in everything else, unite in blind insensibility to appreciate the grandeur of the place Man occupies therein.

Nay, more thoughtful men, once escaped from the blinding influences of traditional prejudice, will find in the lowly stock whence man has sprung the best evidence of the splendour of his capacities; and will discern in his long progress through the Past, a reasonable ground of faith in his attainment of a nobler Future.

They will remember that in comparing civilized man with the animal world, one is as the Alpine traveller, who sees the mountains soaring into the sky and can hardly discern where the deep shadowed crags and roseate peaks end, and where the clouds of heaven begin. Surely the awe-struck voyager may be excused if, at first, he refuses to believe the geologist, who tells him that these glorious masses are, after all, the hardened mud of primeval seas, or the cooled slag of subterranean furnaces—of one substance with the dullest clay, but raised by inward forces to that place of proud and seemingly inaccessible glory.

But the geologist is right; and due reflection on his teachings, instead of diminishing our reverence and our wonder, adds all the force of intellectual sublimity to the mere esthetic intuition of the uninstructed beholder.

And after passion and prejudice have died away, the same result will attend the teachings of the naturalist respecting that great Alps and Andes of the living world—Man. Our reverence for the nobility of manhood will not be lessened by the knowledge that Man is, in substance and in structure, one with the brutes; for he alone possesses the marvellous endowment of intelligible and rational speech, whereby, in the secular period of his existence, he has slowly accumulated and organized the experience which is almost wholly lost with the cessation of every individual life in other animals; so that now he stands raised upon it as on a mountain top, far above the level of his humble fellows, and transfigured from his grosser nature by reflecting, here and there, a ray from the infinite source of truth.

Preview the passage to gain an overview. Then write your answers to the following questions:

- What is the subject of the passage?
- What point is the author making about this subject?

Preview:

Write a brief summary of the passage you just read.

Summary:

Choose the *best* answer to each of the following questions.

1. What is humankind's relation to the lower animals?

   a. They are as much alike as one human is like another; there is no difference.
   b. Humans are superior to the other animals in every way.
   c. They are in substance and structure the same, but humans are raised by the power of speech.
   d. Animals are actually superior to humans in terms of physical strength and base cunning.
   e. Humans are smarter, but animals are stronger.

2. Which humans will recognize the truth of their relation to other species?

    a. the cynics;
    b. the intellectuals and the self-righteous;
    c. the scientists;
    d. the Alpine travellers;
    e. those capable of using an open mind and common-sense.

3. The Alps in this passage represent

    a. both the glory and the base substance of human-kind;
    b. the beauty of nature;
    c. the rocky path of the scientist;
    d. the physical superiority of humans to other animals;
    e. none of the above.

4. According to the passage, the possession of rational speech

    a. places humans further from the lower animals and thus from their natural state;
    b. endows humans with the power to leave others the wisdom of their experience;
    c. hinders humans from communicating in the original, natural mode of the lower animals;
    d. allows humans to communicate;
    e. equalizes the imbalance between human and animal strength.

From "The Method of Scientific Investigation," T. H. Huxley

Prompt: Do you consider yourself a scientist?

You have heard it repeated, I dare say, that men of science work by means of induction and deduction and that, by the help of these operations, they wring from nature certain other things (which are called natural laws and causes), and that out of these, by some cunning skill of their own, they build up hypotheses and theories. And it is imagined by many that the operations of the common mind can be by no means compared with these processes. To hear all these large words, you would think that the mind of a man of science must be constituted differently from that of his fellow men. But if you will not be frightened by terms, you will discover that you are quite wrong, and that all these terrible apparatus are being used by yourself every day of your life.

A very trivial circumstance will serve to exemplify this. Suppose you go into a fruiterer's shop, wanting an apple. You take up one, and on biting it, you find it is sour. You look at it and see that it is hard and green. You take up another one, and that too is hard, green, and sour. The shopman offers you a third; but, before biting it, you examine it and find that it is hard and green, and you immediately say that you will not have it, as it must be sour, like those you have already tried.

Nothing can be more simple than that, you think; but if you will take the trouble to analyze what has been done by your mind, you will be greatly surprised. In the first place, you have performed the operation of induction. You found that, in two experiences, hardness and greenness in apples went together with sourness. It was so in the first case, and it was confirmed by the second. True, it is a very small basis, but still it is enough to make an induction from; you generalize the facts, and you expect to find sourness in apples when you get hardness and greenness. You found upon that a general law—that all hard and green apples are sour; and this, so far as it goes, is a perfect induction.

Well, having got your natural law in this way, when you are offered another apple which you find is hard and green, you say, "All hard and green apples are sour; this apple is hard and green; therefore this apple is sour." That train of reasoning is what we call a syllogism, and has all its various parts and terms—its major premise, its minor premise, and its conclusion—and, by the help of further reasoning, you arrive at your final determination, "I will not have that apple." You see, you have, in the first place, established a law by induction, and upon that you have founded a deduction and reasoned out the special conclusion of the particular case.

Well, now, suppose, having got your law, that at some time afterward you are discussing the qualities of apples with a friend. You say to him, "It is a very curious thing, but I find that all hard and green apples are sour!" Your friend says to you, "But how do you know that?" You at once reply, "Oh, because I have tried them over and over again, and have always found them to be so." Well, if we were talking science instead of common sense, we should call that an experimental verification. And, if still opposed, you go further and say, "I have heard from the people in Somersetshire and Devonshire, where a large number of apples are grown, that they have observed the same thing. It is also found to be the case in Normandy and in North America. In short, I find it to be the universal experience of mankind wherever attention has been directed to the subject." Whereupon your friend, unless he is a very unreasonable man, agrees with you and is convinced that you are quite right in the conclusion you have drawn. He sees that the experiment has been tried under all sorts of conditions as to time, place, and people, with the same results; and he says with you, therefore, that the law you have laid down must be a good one and that he must believe it.

In science we do the same, though in a much more delicate manner. In scientific inquiry it becomes a matter of duty to expose a supposed law to every possible kind of verification and to take care, moreover, that this is done intentionally and not left to a mere accident, as in the case of the apples. And in science, as in common life, our confidence in a law is in exact proportion to the absence of variation in the result of our experimental verifications. For instance, if you let go your grasp of an article that you may have in your hand, it will immediately fall to the ground. This is a very common verification of one of the best established laws of nature—that of gravitation. The method by which men of science establish the existence of that law is exactly the same as that by which we have established the trivial proposition about the sourness of hard and green apples. But we believe it in such an extensive, thorough, and unhesitating manner because the universal experience of mankind verifies it, and we can verify it ourselves at any time; and that is the strongest possible foundation on which any natural law can rest.

Preview the passage to gain an overview. Then write your answers to the following questions:

- What is the subject of the passage?
- What point is the author making about this subject?

Preview:

Write a brief summary of the passage you just read.

Summary:

Choose the *best* answer to each of the following questions.

1. The author suggests that all people

   a. are influenced by scientists;
   b. need formal training in science;
   c. would be better off if they learned the scientific method;
   d. are capable of thinking scientifically.

2. Many people, according to the author, regard scientists

   a. as possessing a special kind of knowledge;
   b. as being just like everyone else;
   c. as heroes of society;
   d. as threats to religion.

3. The author suggests that a person's lack of understanding could result from

   a. a lack of scientific experience;
   b. a fear of big words;
   c. poor schooling;
   d. problems brought on by technology.

4. Induction involves

    a. moving from the general to the particular;

    b. reading the work of great scientists;

    c. moving from the particular to the general;

    d. learning the rules of logic.

5. Deduction means

    a. moving from the general to the particular;

    b. moving from the particular to the general;

    c. learning the rules of logic;

    d. reading the works of the great scientists.

From *The Rules of Sociological Method,* Emile Durkheim

Prompt: What do sociologists do?

Here, then, is a category of facts which present very special characteristics: they consist of manners of acting, thinking and feeling external to the individual, which are invested with a coercive power by virtue of which they exercise control over him. Consequently, since they consist of representations and actions, they cannot be confused with organic phenomena, which have no existence save in and through the individual consciousness. Thus they constitute a new species and to them must be exclusively assigned the term *social*. It is appropriate, since it is clear that, not having the individual as their substratum, they can have none other than society, either political society in its entirety or one of the partial groups that it includes—religious denominations, political and literary schools, occupational corporations, etc. Moreover it is for such as these alone that the term is fitting, for the word "social" has the sole meaning of designating those phenomena which fall into none of the categories of facts already constituted and labelled. They are consequently the proper field of sociology. It is true that this word "constraint," in terms of which we define them, is in danger of infuriating those who zealously uphold out-and-out individualism. Since they maintain that the individual is completely autonomous, it seems to them that he is diminished every time he is made aware that he is not dependent on himself alone. Yet since it is indisputable today that most of our ideas and tendencies are not developed by ourselves, but come to us from outside, they can only penetrate us by imposing themselves upon us. This is all that our definition implies. Moreover we know that all social constraints do not necessarily exclude the individual personality.

Preview the passage to gain an overview. Then write your answers to the following questions:

- What is the subject of the passage?
- What point is the author making about this subject?

Preview:

Write a brief summary of the passage you just read.

Summary:

Choose the *best* answer to each of the following questions.

1. Where, according to the author, do most of our ideas come from?

    a. ourselves;
    b. society;
    c. school;
    d. our parents;
    e. religious authority.

2. In this passage, how is the word "social" defined?

    a. as phenomena consisting of representations and actions;
    b. people-oriented;
    c. as facts which overlap established theoretical categories;
    d. prone to follow established rules;
    e. prone to follow socially accepted, but not enforced, guidelines.

3. What is an example of a "social" fact, as given by the author?

    a. manners of acting, thinking, and feeling which come from outside the individual and have control over that individual;
    b. manners of acting, thinking, and feeling which are exclusively produced within the individual;
    c. manners of acting which come from outside an individual, but exercise no control over that individual;
    d. manners of thinking which come from one area of an individual 's life and seem to come from an internal source;
    e. manners of thinking which the individual acknowledges as external but are, in fact, internal.

4. Why would the author's stated tenets infuriate advocates of extreme individualism?

    a. The author assumes that all ideas come from outside the individual, and the self produces no tendencies valuable in everyday life.

    b. The author implies that the individual is the most important building block of society.

    c. The author implies nothing that would upset or challenge individualists.

    d. The author proposes that the individual develops ideas and tendencies which are imposed from outside the self.

    e. The author proposes that the individual is fully autonomous.

From "A Summary View of the Principle of Population," Thomas Malthus

Prompt: How big a threat is the population explosion?

But if the natural increase of population, when unchecked by the difficulty of procuring the means of subsistence or other peculiar causes, be such as to continue doubling its numbers in twenty-five years, and if the greatest increase of food which, for a continuance, could possibly take place on a limited territory like our earth in its present state, at the most only such as would add every twenty-five years an amount equal to its present produce, then it is quite clear that a powerful check on the increase of population must be almost constantly in action.

By the laws of nature man cannot live without food. Whatever may be the rate at which population would increase if unchecked, it never can actually increase in any country beyond the food necessary to support it. But by the laws of nature in respect to the powers of a limited territory, the additions which can be made in equal periods to the food which it produces must, after a short time, either be constantly decreasing, which is what would really take place, or, at the very most, must remain stationary so as to increase the means of subsistence only in an arithmetical progression. Consequently, it follows necessarily that the average rate of the *actual* increase of population over the greatest part of the globe, obeying the same laws as the increase of food, must be totally of a different character from the rate at which it would increase if *unchecked*.

The great question, then, which remains to be considered, is the manner in which this constant and necessary check upon population practically operates.

Preview the passage to gain an overview. Then write your answers to the following questions:

- What is the subject of the passage?
- What point is the author making about this subject?

Preview:

Write a brief summary of the passage you just read.

Summary:

Choose the *best* answer to each of the following questions.

1. Why is it clear, according to the author, that there is a check on population?

    a. It is not clear that a check exists, because the population doubles every 25 years.
    b. Unchecked, the natural increase of the population would continuously be doubling its numbers every 25 years, and this is not the case.
    c. It is not clear, although the population does not double every 25 years.
    d. Unchecked, the natural increase of the population would be only slight and, therefore, manageable.
    e. None of the above answers is applicable to this passage.

2. What is the check on the population that keeps the numbers down?

    a. war;
    b. pestilence;
    c. the amount of people living in one area in a single period of time;
    d. disease;
    e. the amount of available food corresponding to the existing population.

3. In the last sentence of this passage, what does the author mean by "practically operates"?

    a. the theoretical application of the practical examples he has offered;
    b. the application of his theory in the "real" world;
    c. the seeming operation of the hypothesis he has given;
    d. the practical nature of the theory he espouses;
    e. practically operating, but not actually operating.

4. What alternative does this passage offer to compensate for the natural check on population?

   a. reform the global system of agriculture;
   b. investigate the root causes of epidemic illnesses;
   c. research food distribution throughout developing countries;
   d. the passage offers no alternative to the natural check on population;
   e. work toward a united relief effort for populations hit hardest by famine and drought.

From *The Ego and the Id,* Sigmund Freud

Prompt: What role does the subconscious play in your
behavior?

"Being conscious" is in the first place a purely descriptive term,
resting on perception of the most immediate and certain character. Experience goes on to show that a psychical element (for
instance, an idea) is not as a rule conscious for a protracted
length of time. On the contrary, a state of consciousness is char-
acteristically very transitory; an idea that is conscious now is
no longer so a moment later, although it can become so again
under certain conditions that are easily brought about. In the
interval the idea was—we do not know what. We can say that it
was *latent,* and by this we mean that it was *capable of becoming
conscious* at any time. Or, if we say that it was *unconscious,* we
shall also be giving a correct description of it. Here "unconscious"
coincides with "latent, and capable of becoming conscious." The
philosophers would no doubt object: "No, the term 'unconscious'
is not applicable here; so long as the idea was in a state of la-
tency it was not anything psychical at all." To contradict them
at this point would lead to nothing more profitable than a ver-
bal dispute.

But we have arrived at the term or concept of the unconscious
along another path, by considering certain experiences in which
mental *dynamics* play a part. We have found—that is, we have
been obliged to assume—that very powerful mental processes
or ideas exist (and here a quantitative or *economic* factor comes
into question for the first time) which can produce all the effects
in mental life that ordinary ideas do (including effects that can
in their turn become conscious as ideas), though they themselves
do not become conscious.

Preview the passage to gain an overview. Then write your answers to the following questions:

- What is the subject of the passage?
- What point is the author making about this subject?

Preview:

Write a brief summary of the passage you just read.

Summary:

Choose the *best* answer to each of the following questions.

1. What does the author mean by the term "latent" idea?

   a. an idea, not yet conscious, but with the potential to be conscious at any time;
   b. an idea that came into being too late to be of use;
   c. an idea that is already a conscious thought;
   d. an idea that was conscious and is no longer so;
   e. b and d.

2. What does the author cite as the evidence that an idea is not always conscious for a protracted length of time?

   a. psychological studies;
   b. biological facts;
   c. statistical data;
   d. experience;
   e. personal feeling.

3. According to the passage, is an "unconscious" idea known to the individual to whom it belongs?

   a. yes, although the individual is unaware of knowing this information;
   b. no, not until the idea becomes "conscious";
   c. no, not until the idea becomes "latent";
   d. yes, because "unconscious" is merely a descriptive term;
   e. no, because "idea" is merely a descriptive term.

4. In the author's view, what proves the existence of unconscious mental ideas and processes in quantitative terms?

   a. There is no proof.
   b. The author uses personal experience as proof.
   c. Unconscious ideas produce all the same effects in mental life that ordinary ideas produce.
   d. Unconscious ideas produce different and often mutated effects in mental life, as opposed to the effects ordinary ideas produce.
   e. He measures the exact effects unconscious ideas produce.

Readings in Humanities

Until recently, the readings on the ACT, the SAT, and similar tests were almost always nonfictional passages selected for tests. Currently, however, the ACT always includes a selection from a short story or novel and the SAT and other tests regularly include literature. In addition, many of the newer tests have incorporated poems and scenes from plays as well as works of prose fiction.

You should not be surprised, then, to encounter on an achievement test a work of fiction and associated questions such as the following:

- What is the theme?
- What contributes to the mood?
- What can we conclude about the characters?
- What might happen next in the story?
- Which writing techniques do you recognize in the author's work?

These questions evaluate your ability to analyze a piece of literature. No doubt you are asked similar questions in your English class. In fact, you may ask yourself the same sort of questions indirectly as you decide whether you liked a movie you saw with your friends or a suspenseful mystery you read for pleasure.

Analysis of poetry, in particular, calls for an understanding of some specific terminology. Though most of the questions following a poem will concern its meaning, you are likely to encounter some questions that require you to understand poetic terminology. Here are a few terms that you are expected to know and be able to apply in your analysis:

- **alliteration**—the repetition of consonant sounds at the beginning of words
- **allusion**—a reference to historical, mythological, biblical, or other bodies of knowledge outside the work.
- **ambiguity**—double or multiple meanings.

- **apostrophe**—calling out to a dead or imaginary person.
- **connotation**—the suggested meaning of a word or phrase.
- **couplet**—two consecutive lines of poetry that rhyme.
- **figurative language**—expressions that make comparisons meant to be taken imaginatively and not literally; the most common are

  simile—a comparison using *like* or *as*.

  metaphor—an implied comparison.

  personification—giving human qualities to a nonhuman.
- **form**—the organizing principle that shapes a work. Some of the most common are:

  ballad—a poem relating a dramatic story.

  haiku—a short lyric poem that conveys an image. The poem is presented in three lines of five, seven, and five syllables, respectively.

  lyric—a short personal poem expressing emotions and thoughts.

  ode—a lyric poem written to praise someone or something.

  sonnet—a fourteen-line lyric poem with rigid rhyme scheme and organization.

  villanelle—a lyric poem made of five stanzas of three lines (*aba* rhyme scheme) plus a final stanza of four lines (*abaa*).
- **hyperbole**—exaggeration or overstatement.
- **imagery**—language referring to something that can be perceived through one or more of the senses.
- **meter**—the fixed pattern of accented and unaccented syllables.
- **mood**—the prevailing emotional attitude.
- **paradox**—an apparently self-contradictory statement.
- **persona**—the voice of the poem's narrator.
- **rhyme scheme**—the patterns of rhymes in a stanza.
- **symbol**—something concrete that stands for something abstract.
- **theme**—the central or dominating idea.
- **tone**—the poet's attitude toward the subject.

SOME GUIDELINES

Before you continue your strategic reading practice, try these exercises. They should help you focus upon specific aspects of the literature. You might even find that this approach to analysis helps to give you ideas for original stories for writing assignments.

Think about plot:

1. List books with the following kinds of plots.

    Complex
    Subtle
    Chronological
    Nonchronological

2. Relate a personal incident that reveals one of your most essential character traits. Next, relate it a second time, using a flashback.

Think about character:

1. List your favorite characters from literature. What qualities do these characters have in common? How do these characters affect outcome in the books?

2. Describe a real person who has influenced you. How would you develop that person's character in your writing?

Think about theme:

1. List novels, stories, plays, or poems that convey these themes:

    Love has the power to heal.
    Life is full of illusions.
    Life is fair.
    Life is not fair.
    Experience teaches important lessons.

2. For each theme listed above, write a fable that uses the theme as its moral.

Think about setting:

1. List novels or stories whose settings were essential to the characters and the story.

2. Describe some techniques writers can use to convey information about setting.

Remember to practice the three steps to strategic reading:

1. Preview before you read.
2. Underline and annotate while you read.
3. Summarize after you read.

"To Solitude," John Keats

Prompt: Describe a time you enjoyed being alone.

O Solitude! If I must with thee dwell,
Let it not be among the jumbled heap
Of murky buildings, climb with me the steep,—
Nature's observatory—whence the dell,
Its flowery slopes, its river's crystal swell,
May seem a span; let me thy vigils keep
'Mongst boughs pavillion'd, where the deer's swift leap
Startles the wild bee from the fox-glove bell.
But though I'll gladly trace these scenes with thee,
Yet the sweet converse of an innocent mind,
Whose words are images of thoughts refin'd,
Is my soul's pleasure; and it sure must be
Almost the highest bliss of human-kind,
When to thy haunts two kindred spirits flee.

Preview the poem to gain an overview. Then write your answers
to the following questions:

- What is the subject of the poem?
- What point is the author making about this subject?

Preview:

Write a brief summary of the poem you just read.

Summary:

Choose the *best* answer to each of the following questions.

1. This poem is an example of a

   a. ballad;
   b. rondo;
   c. haiku;
   d. sonnet.

2.   The poet views the city as

a.   inferior to the country;
b.   a profound mystery;
c.   potentially inspiring;
d.   the best place to write poetry.

3.   The poet suggests that loneliness is

a.   more common in the modern world;
b.   unavoidable;
c.   a weakness;
d.   potentially inspiring.

4.   The "highest bliss" can be attained when

a.   nature is controlled;
b.   people accept their destiny;
c.   two people enjoy nature together;
d.   cities are destroyed.

5.   In line 9 "thee" refers to

a.   the poet's lover;
b.   nature;
c.   solitude;
d.   the poet's friend.

From *The Picture of Dorian Gray,* Oscar Wilde

Prompt: How do you define "beauty"?

"But beauty, real beauty, ends where an intellectual expression begins. Intellect is in itself a mode of exaggeration, and destroys the harmony of any face. The moment one sits down to think, one becomes all nose, or all forehead, or something horrid. Look at the successful men in any of the learned professions. How perfectly hideous they are! Except, of course, in the Church. But then in the Church they don't think. A bishop keeps on saying at the age of eighty what he was told to say when he was a boy of eighteen, and as a natural consequence he always looks absolutely delightful. Your mysterious young friend, whose name you have never told me, but whose picture really fascinates me, never thinks. I feel quite sure of that. He is some brainless, beautiful creature, who should be always here in winter when we have no flowers to look at, and always here in summer when we want something to chill our intelligence. Don't flatter yourself, Basil: you are not in the least like him."

"You don't understand me, Harry," answered the artist. "Of course I am not like him. I know that perfectly well. Indeed, I should be sorry to look like him. You shrug your shoulders? I am telling you the truth. There is a fatality about all physical and intellectual distinction, the sort of fatality that seems to dog through history the faltering steps of kings. It is better not to be different from one's fellows. The ugly and the stupid have the best of it in this world. They can sit at their ease and gape at the play. If they know nothing of victory, they are at least spared the knowledge of defeat. They live as we all should live, undisturbed, indifferent, and without disquiet. They neither bring ruin upon others, nor ever receive it from alien hands. Your rank and wealth, Harry; my brains such as they are—my art, whatever it may be worth; Dorian Gray's good looks—we shall all suffer for what the gods have given us, suffer terribly"

Preview the passage to gain an overview. Then write your answers to the following questions:

- What is the subject of the passage?
- What point is the author making about this subject?

Preview:

Write a brief summary of the passage you just read.

Summary:

Choose the *best* answer to each of the following questions.

1. What might the cynical attitudes of the speakers hide?

    a. the real wish to be ugly and stupid;

    b. the real wish to be beautiful or brilliant themselves;

    c. a longing for more beautiful and stupid individuals to amuse them;

    d. a longing for more ugly and brilliant people to keep their minds occupied;

    e. the speakers showed no cynicism by their remarks.

2. Who, according to Basil, has it best in this world?

    a. the ugly and stupid;

    b. the beautiful and talented;

    c. the intelligent and motivated;

    d. the artistic and creative;

    e. Basil believes everyone has his or her share of suffering.

3. What, according to Harry, ruins real beauty?

    a. perfect symmetry of features, because each face should have some character to it;

    b. the intellect, because no one can see past the speaker's words to appreciate the beauty on its own terms;

    c. a religious affiliation, because beauty is wasted in a clerical capacity;

    d. youth, because he believes beauty is only enhanced by wisdom and experience;

    e. intellect, because it destroys the harmony of a face.

4. Why, as stated in the passage, is it better *not* to be different from other people?

    a. Unimpressive and average individuals can live without being bothered, defeated, or upset because they never bother, defeat, or upset others.
    b. The ugly and stupid can enjoy the benefits of other people's pity.
    c. Unimpressive and average individuals can live without the consequences of disturbing others because no one suspects them.
    d. Most people avoid the beautiful and brilliant because they are different from everyone else.
    e. To be an average individual is to taste the sweetest victories by exceeding others' expectations.

From *Anna Karenina,* Leo Tolstoy

Prompt: What makes a family happy?

Happy families are all alike; every unhappy family is unhappy in its own way.

Everything was in confusion in the Oblonskys' house. The wife had discovered that the husband was carrying on an intrigue with a French girl, who had been a governess in their family, and she had announced to her husband that she could not go on living in the same house with him. This position of affairs had now lasted three days, and not only the husband and wife themselves, but all the members of their family and household, were painfully conscious of it. Every person in the house felt that there was no sense in their living together, and that the stray people brought together by chance in any inn had more in common with one another than they, the members of the family and household of the Oblonskys. The wife did not leave her own room, the husband had not been at home in three days. The children ran wild all over the house; the English governess quarreled with the housekeeper, and wrote to a friend asking her to look out for a new situation for her; the man-cook had walked off the day before just at dinner-time; the kitchen-maid and the coachman had given warning.

Preview the passage to gain an overview. Then write your answers to the following questions:

- What is the subject of the passage?
- What point is the author making about this subject?

Preview:

Write a brief summary of the passage you just read.

Summary:

Choose the *best* answer to each of the following questions.

1. Why are the Oblonskys unhappy?

    a. They are at a loss for what to do now that the servants have quit.
    b. The semblance of a happy family has been disrupted by a divorce.
    c. The semblance of a happy family has been disrupted by the discovery of adultery.
    d. The favorite middle child has run away from home.
    e. The servants have decided to run the household without advice from their employers.

2. From what point of view is this passage written?

    a. omniscient;
    b. first person;
    c. personal;
    d. second person;
    e. impossible to tell from this passage alone.

3. Which of the following clues included in this passage is *not* representative of the family's social class?

    a. the abundance of servants;
    b. the separate rooms for husband and wife;
    c. the presence of a governess;
    d. the enormous landed estate where they reside;
    e. The passage gives no clues about the family's class background.

4. What is one of the symbols of the household's state of confusion?

    a. The house itself is under construction.
    b. The mother and father continually quarrel with their children.
    c. The mother and father forgot they have children.
    d. The husband had not been home for three days.
    e. The family's business interests have suffered considerably.

From *Emma,* Jane Austen

Prompt: What happens if people always get their own way?

Sixteen years had Miss Taylor been in Mr. Woodhouse's family, less as a governess than a friend, very fond of both daughters, but particularly of Emma. Between *them* it was more the intimacy of sisters. Even before Miss Taylor had ceased to hold the nominal office of governess, the mildness of her temper had hardly allowed her to impose any restraint; and the shadow of authority being now long passed away, they had been living together as friend and friend very mutually attached, and Emma doing just what she liked; highly esteeming Miss Taylor's judgment, but directed chiefly by her own.

The real evils indeed of Emma's situation were the power of having rather too much her own way, and a disposition to think a little too well of herself; these were the disadvantages which threatened alloy to her many enjoyments. The danger, however, was at present, so unperceived, that they did not by any means rank as misfortunes with her.

Sorrow came—a gentle sorrow—but not at all in the shape of any disagreeable consciousness. Miss Taylor married. It was Miss Taylor's loss which first brought grief.

Preview the passage to gain an overview. Then write your answers to the following questions:

- What is the subject of the passage?
- What point is the author making about this subject?

Preview:

Write a brief summary of the passage you just read.

Summary:

Choose the *best* answer to each of the following questions.

1. What is Miss Taylor's relation to Emma?

   a. governess;
   b. sister;
   c. mother;
   d. mentor;
   e. English teacher.

2. What is the "real evil" in Emma's life?

   a. Miss Taylor's marriage;
   b. Emma's conflict with her father;
   c. Emma's lack of wealth and position;
   d. Emma's pernicious character;
   e. the power Emma had of always getting her own way.

3. How can it be inferred that Miss Taylor caused Emma unhappiness?

   a. She has married and thus must move out of the Woodhouses' residence.
   b. She has grieved her by leaving without provocation.
   c. She has quarreled with Emma.
   d. She has unfairly judged Emma for not getting married herself.
   e. Miss Taylor inadvertently caused Emma grief by allowing her to do whatever she pleased.

4. In speaking of Emma, what kind of tone does the author employ?

   a. awestruck;
   b. ironic;
   c. bitter;
   d. cynical;
   e. admiring.

"O World," George Santayana

Prompt: Is a knowledgeable person necessarily a wise person?

O world, thou choosest not the better part!
It is not wisdom to be only wise,
And on the inward vision close the eyes,
But it is wisdom to believe the heart.
Columbus found a world, and had no chart,
Save one that faith deciphered in the skies;
To trust the soul's invincible surmise
Was all his science and his only art.
Our knowledge is a torch of smoky pine
That lights the pathway but one step ahead
Across a void of mystery and dread.
Bid, then, the tender light of faith to shine
By which alone the mortal heart is led
Unto the thinking of the thought divine.

Preview the poem to gain an overview. Then write your answers to the following questions:

- What is the subject of the poem?
- What point is the author making about this subject?

Preview:

Write a brief summary of the poem you just read.

Summary:

Choose the *best* answer to each of the following questions.

1. What is the poet suggesting about human knowledge?
    a. It is limited.
    b. We can understand some things better than others.
    c. We know ourselves better than we know the world.
    d. We need to keep developing it.

2. "Our knowledge is a torch . . ." is an example of

    a. personification;
    b. apostrophe;
    c. metaphor;
    d. allusion.

3. Columbus proves that

    a. we can succeed without knowledge;
    b. formal education is essential for success;
    c. Europeans understand the relationship between thinking and feeling;
    d. we must respond to our feelings first.

4. "It is not wisdom to be only wise" is an example of

    a. simile;
    b. personification;
    c. hyperbole;
    d. paradox.

5. Who might disagree with this poem?

    a. a minister;
    b. an atheist scientist;
    c. an artist;
    d. a laborer.

"What Mystery Pervades a Well!"
Emily Dickinson

Prompt: When are you reminded that much of life is
mysterious?

What mystery pervades a well!
The water lives so far—
A neighbor from another world
Residing in a jar.

Whose limit none have ever seen,
But just his lid of glass—
Like looking every time you please
In an abyss's face!

The grass does not appear afraid,
I often wonder he
Can stand so close and look so bold
At what is awe to me.

Related somehow they may be,
The sedge stands next the sea—
Where he is floorless, and of fear
No evidence gives he.

But nature is a stranger yet;
The ones that cite her most
Have never passed her haunted house,
Nor simplified her ghost.

To pity those that know her not
Is helped by the regret
That those who know her, know her less
The nearer her they get.

Preview the poem to gain an overview. Then write your answers
to the following questions:

- What is the subject of the poem?
- What point is the author making about this subject?

Preview:

Write a brief summary of the poem you just read.

Summary:

Choose the *best* answer to each of the following questions.

1. The poet suggests that the more we know about nature, the

   a. less we understand;
   b. more we appreciate her;
   c. more we believe in God;
   d. more we see ourselves.

2. The poet uses personification to characterize

   a. water;
   b. grass;
   c. sedge;
   d. all of the above.

3. The best meaning for "abyss" is

   a. valley;
   b. bottomless pit;
   c. rock formation;
   d. cloud.

4. The mood of the poem is

   a. upbeat;
   b. zealous;
   c. gloomy;
   d. fitful.

5. The "ones who cite her most" are those who

   a. study nature from afar;
   b. adore nature;
   c. paint nature;
   d. fear nature.

From *Great Expectations,* Charles Dickens

Prompt: What can you learn about a person from his or her eating habits?

Mr. Pumblechook and I breakfasted at eight o'clock in the parlor behind the shop, while the shopman took his mug of tea and lunch of bread-and-butter on a sack of peas in the front premises. I considered Mr. Pumblechook wretched company. Besides being possessed by my sister's idea that a mortifying and penitential character ought to be imparted to my diet—besides giving me as much crumb as possible in combination with as little butter, and putting such a quantity of warm water into my milk that it would have been more candid to have left the milk out altogether—his conversation consisted of nothing but arithmetic. On my politely bidding him Good morning, he said, pompously, "Seven times nine, boy?" And how should *I* be able to answer, dodged in that way, in a strange place, on an empty stomach! I was hungry, but before I had swallowed a morsel, he began a running sum that lasted all through the breakfast. "Seven?" "and four?" "and eight?" "And six?" "And two?" "And ten?" And so on. And after each figure was disposed of, it was as much as I could do to get a bite or a sup, before the next came; while he sat at his ease guessing nothing, and eating bacon and hot roll, in (if I may be allowed the expression) a gorging and gormandising manner.

Preview the passage to gain an overview. Then write your answers to the following questions:

- What is the subject of the passage?
- What point is the author making about this subject?

Preview:

Write a brief summary of the passage you just read.

Summary:

Choose the *best* answer to each of the following questions.

1. What do the contents of the different breakfasts illustrate about Pumblechook?

    a. Pumblechook thinks the narrator needs to watch what he eats, so he gives him small portions of food.
    b. Pumblechook is a hypocrite who employs a double standard, as evidenced by the discrepancy between his meal and the boy's.
    c. Pumblechook really believes that meager rations will make the boy a stronger person.
    d. Pumblechook thinks adults need more sustenance than children do.
    e. The difference in their breakfasts has no meaning that the reader can determine from this passage.

2. What kind of tone does the narrator use to make his point about Pumblechook?

    a. The narrator uses a mocking, pointed tone to portray Pumblechook's shortcomings.
    b. The narrator sounds respectful and humble about Pumblechook's exalted position.
    c. The tone is affectionate and playful.
    d. The narrator's tone illustrates the typical strained relationship between an adult and a child.
    e. The tone betrays the slavish idolatry Pumblechook is usually accorded.

3. How does this passage portray a child's perspective?

    a. This passage describes how a young person views the unfairness and condescension in his relationship with certain adults.
    b. This passage allows a glimpse into how children of this era often respect and obey their elders without question.
    c. On the whole, children enjoy being disciplined even though they pretend to despise the process.
    d. The passage reveals the dynamics of both an immature and mature mind in conversation.
    e. This passage represents the fear and intimidation of authority figures that most children experience.

4. How does Pumblechook feel about children in general, as evidenced by his treatment of the narrator?

   a. Pumblechook shows his consideration and respect for the child's intelligence by his mathematics questions.

   b. Pumblechook tries to hide his affection for the child beneath a layer of well-meant, but brusque, authoritative behavior.

   c. Pumbelchook thinks of children as inferiors and acts uncomfortable and unnatural in an effort to appear superior.

   d. Pumblechook coddles children by refusing to allow them any hardship or discomfort.

   e. Pumblechook relates poorly to children because of his high-level intelligence and position.

From "The Minister's Black Veil," Nathaniel Hawthorne

Prompt: What does a black veil symbolize to you?

Father Hooper's breath heaved; it rattled in his throat; but, with a mighty effort, grasping forward with his hands, he caught hold of life, and held it back till he should speak. He even raised himself in bed; and there he sat, shivering with the arms of death around him, while the black veil hung down, awful, at that last moment, in the gathered terrors of a lifetime. And yet the faint, sad smile, so often there, now seemed to glimmer from its obscurity, and linger on Father Hooper's lips.

"Why do you tremble at me alone?" cried he, turning his veiled face round the circle of pale spectators. "Tremble also at each other! Have men avoided me, and women shown no pity, and children screamed and fled, only for my black veil? What, but the mystery which it obscurely typifies, has made this piece of crape so awful? When the friend shows his inmost heart to his friend; the lover to his best beloved; when man does not vainly shrink from the eye of his Creator, loathsomely treasuring up the secret of his sin; then deem me a monster, for the symbol beneath which I have lived, and die! I look around me, and, lo! on every visage a Black Veil!"

While his auditors shrank from one another, in mutual affront, Father Hooper fell back upon his pillow, a veiled corpse, with a faint smile lingering on the lips. Still veiled, they laid him in his coffin, and a veiled corpse they bore him to the grave. The grass of many years has sprung up and withered on the grave, the burial stone is moss-grown, and good Mr. Hooper's face is dust; but awful is still the thought that it mouldered beneath the Black Veil!

Preview the passage to gain an overview. Then write your answers to the following questions:

- What is the subject of the passage?
- What point is the author making about this subject?

Preview:

Write a brief summary of the passage you just read.

Summary:

Choose the *best* answer to each of the following questions.

1. What object in the passage is directly symbolized by the veil?

   a. Father Hooper's deformity;
   b. Puritan ideals;
   c. no object is directly symbolized, but the veil represents a mystery inexplicable to its viewers;
   d. Father Hooper's loneliness and desperation;
   e. no object is directly symbolized, but the reader can infer that the veil represents the suffering of humankind.

2. Why does his speech frighten Father Hooper's listeners?

   a. He reminds his listeners that they all will be judged, although more fairly than they have judged him.
   b. He reminds his listeners that they each wear an actual black veil similar to his.
   c. He scares his listeners by bringing up their past conduct and threatening them with the legal consequences.
   d. He scares his listeners by revealing the true secret he keeps behind his veil.
   e. Although he attempts to frighten them, his listeners are merely giving an appropriate response to his speech in order to humor a dying man.

3. Why, as portrayed in this passage, have the majority of the townspeople scorned him?

   a. He is horribly disfigured.
   b. The veil is a symbol of disgrace and penalty.
   c. They are afraid of the mystery typified by the veil.
   d. They are afraid of what they cannot explain.
   e. c and d.

4. Why, can you infer, is Father Hooper smiling as he raises himself from his deathbed?

    a. He feels victorious over those around him and justified in his actions.
    b. He is under the delusion that he will be cured.
    c. He is asking for forgiveness from his friends for his wrongdoing.
    d. He must be feeling relieved to have so many loved ones around him at the end.
    e. Nothing can be inferred from the above passage about Father Hooper's behavior.

From *Middlemarch,* George Eliot

Prompt: How does change in a relationship seem like betrayal?

Poor Mr. Casaubon! This suffering was the harder to bear because it seemed like a betrayal: the young creature who had worshipped him with perfect trust had quickly turned into the critical wife; and early instances of criticism and resentment had made an impression which no tenderness and submission afterwards could remove. To his suspicious interpretation Dorothea's silence now was a suppressed rebellion; a remark from her which he had not in any way anticipated was an assertion of conscious superiority; her gentle answers had an irritating cautiousness in them; and when she acquiesced it was a self-approved effort of forbearance. The tenacity with which he strove to hide this inward drama made it the more vivid for him; as we hear with the more keenness what we wish others not to hear.

Instead of wondering at this result of misery in Mr. Casaubon, I think it quite ordinary. Will not a tiny speck very close to our vision blot out the glory of the world, and leave only a margin by which we see the blot? I know no speck so troublesome as self. And who, if Mr. Casaubon had chosen to expand his discontent—his suspicions that he was not any longer adored without criticism—could have denied that they were founded on good reasons? On the contrary, there was a strong reason to be added, which he had not himself taken explicitly into account—namely, that he was not unmixedly adorable. He suspected this, however, as he suspected other things, without confessing it, and like the rest of us, felt how soothing it would have been to have a companion who would never find it out.

Preview the passage to gain an overview. Then write your answers to the following questions:

- What is the subject of the passage?
- What point is the author making about this subject?

Preview:

Write a brief summary of the passage you just read.

Summary:

Choose the *best* answer to each of the following questions.

1. Why, as indicated by the passage, is Casaubon so miserable?

    a. because his wife committed adultery;
    b. because his wife has recognized the flaws in his character and no longer idolizes him;
    c. because he is old and sick;
    d. because he has recognized his wife's true character and no longer worships her;
    e. because he feels betrayed by everyone around him.

2. According to the author, what does the speck that interferes with an individual's perspective symbolize?

    a. love;
    b. hope;
    c. self;
    d. knowledge;
    e. truth.

3. What kind of tone does the narrator employ when describing Casaubon's plight?

    a. sympathetic;
    b. honest;
    c. ironic;
    d. understanding;
    e. b, c, and d.

4. Mr. Casaubon would have preferred a mate who

    a. makes him a better person;
    b. lies about his faults;
    c. cannot spot his faults;
    d. lives a hectic life;
    e. none of the above.

From "The Poetic Principle," Edgar Allan Poe

Prompt: How do you define "beauty"? What do your favorite poems have in common?

I would define, in brief, the Poetry of words as *The Rhythmical Creation of Beauty.* Its sole arbiter is Taste. With the Intellect or with the Conscience, it has only collateral relations. Unless incidentally, it has no concern whatever either with Duty or with Truth.

A few words, however, in explanation. *That* pleasure which is at once the most pure, the most elevating, and the most intense, is derived, I maintain, from the contemplation of the Beautiful. In the contemplation of Beauty we alone find it possible to attain that pleasurable elevation, or excitement, *of the soul,* which we recognize as the Poetic Sentiment, and which is so easily distinguished from Truth, which is the satisfaction of the Reason, or from Passion, which is the excitement of the heart. I make Beauty, therefore—using the word as inclusive of the sublime—I make Beauty the province of the poem, simply because it is an obvious rule of Art that effects should be made to spring as directly as possible from their causes—no one as yet having been weak enough to deny that the peculiar elevation in question is at least *most readily* attainable in the poem. It by no means follows, however, that the incitements of Passion, or the precepts of Duty, or even the lessons of Truth, may not be introduced into a poem, and with advantage; for they may subserve, incidentally, in various ways, the general purposes of the work:—but the true artist will always contrive to tone them down in proper subjection to that *Beauty* which is the atmosphere and the real essence of the poem. . . .

Preview the passage to gain an overview. Then write your answers to the following questions:

- What is the subject of the passage?
- What point is the author making about this subject?

Preview:

Write a brief summary of the passage you just read.

Summary:

Choose the *best* answer for each of the following questions.

1. The author's purpose is to show the relationship between

   a. beauty and poetry;
   b. an individual and society;
   c. modern and classical poetry;
   d. personal and popular society.

2. In poetry, according to Poe, appeals to the emotions and to reason

   a. should never appear;
   b. can appear, but should be toned down;
   c. can appear, but never together;
   d. tend to heighten our sense of beauty.

3. Poe suggests that the contemplation of beauty is

   a. possible only with poetry;
   b. possible especially, but not exclusively, with poetry;
   c. a luxury reserved for the wealthy;
   d. a skill only a few can develop.

4. The author assumes

   a. the purposes of poetry will change;
   b. all poets want to recreate scenes of great beauty;
   c. most readers appreciate beauty;
   d. music is the highest form of art.

5. In this selection the author does not

   a. provide a particular instance of beauty;
   b. distinguish among purposes for writing poetry;
   c. gain inspiration from beauty;
   d. regard Truth as subservient to Beauty in poetry.

Answer Key

Social Studies

page 9, Thoreau

1. a.
2. d. Throughout the passage he suggests that people have the choice to improve. It's within their power.
3. b.
4. b. "Where he lives no fugitive slave laws are passed." The "he" refers to the person living in the present. A person in the past would want to pass such laws.
5. a.

page 11, Macaulay

1. c. In the first paragraph, he asks the reader to look back 160 years to the year 1685.
2. c. The text mentions that "some frightful diseases" have disappeared, that the "term of human life has been lengthened," and that the market can be reached in one hour instead of one day.
3. b.
4. d. He cites statistics on mortality rates; uses details such as bricks, scaffolds, and sweepers; and names people like Ormond and Clayton. He does not refer to any studies, however.
5. a.

page 14, Machiavelli

1. c. He states that there is "greater security in being feared than in being loved."
2. e.
3. a. In this passage, he asserts without supplying specific fact.
4. a. He states that people are "covetous of gain."
5. b. He is clearly giving advice to people who want to use this knowledge to gain and keep power.

page 17, Mill

1. c. The last sentence tells us that the individual is "sovereign."
2. a. See line 5.
3. e. See line 10.
4. e. See line 16.

page 19, Bryan

1. d. In the last paragraph, he says, "I am in favor of an income tax."
2. b. In the third paragraph, he states, "They say we passed an unconstitutional law."
3. d.
4. a. In the last paragraph, he says that a tax places "burdens of government justly upon the backs of the people."

page 22, Thucydides

1. b. See lines 4–6.
2. d. The last sentence of the first paragraph states this.
3. e. The second paragraph states the other four reasons. There is no mention anywhere about the neighbor's lack of military skill or might.
4. a. See lines 1–2.

page 25, Lloyd

1. a. Lloyd, in the second paragraph, blames "syndicates and trusts and combinations" for the working person's problems.
2. e. He argues in the first paragraph that people originally had all they needed.
3. d. Government is the only institution of the four that is not blamed.
4. b.

page 27, Locke

1. a. In line 10 he states, "having provided a legislature with power . . ."
2. c. In the first sentence, he states that power, which originates with the individual, is sacrificed to create a community.
3. a. See lines 8–9.
4. c. See the last eight lines.

page 30, Paine and Seabury

1. c. Some will "shrink from service" while others will stand up and fight.
2. b. At the end of the first paragraph he states that "so unlimited a power can belong only to God."

3. d. In the second paragraph he suggests that advances, like the ones in the Jerseys, could have been "repulsed."
4. a. This view is stated in the third paragraph.
5. b. One example is "Tyranny, like hell," a simile.
6. b. See the end of the first paragraph.
7. a. The "you" he addresses believes in natural rights of the colonists. (See lines 1–2.)
8. c.
9. d. In the last paragraph he argues that "independency" and "colony" convey contradictory ideas.
10. c. See the last sentence of the passage.
11. a. Paine sees God as the ultimate source, while Seabury sees the existing government of England as the source of power.
12. a. Seabury is afraid of "man in a state of nature" —confusion, violence, etc.
13. d. Both claim to be for individual rights and freedoms.

Science

page 35, Miller
1. b. See lines 1–8.
2. a. The last sentence states this.
3. e.
4. c.

page 38, Darwin
1. a. The second sentence states this.
2. e. In the third sentence, he says this directly.
3. b. He explains this in the sixth sentence.
4. c. This is stated in the fourth sentence.

page 40, Darwin
1. a. He uses the term to show that humans have replicated natural selection.
2. a. In the third sentence he states how strong the hereditary tendency is.
3. c. The first sentence in the second paragraph makes this point.
4. b.

page 43, Darwin
1. b. The implication is a humanlike ape doing humanlike things. The root also suggests the meaning.
2. b. The first paragraph describes the imagined thoughts of an ape.
3. d. "... he could use stones for fighting and for breaking open nuts ..."

4. c. The end of the first paragraph refers to a human's "disinterested love for all living creatures, the most noble attribute of man. . . ."
5. d. The last three lines state this.

page 46, Huxley
1. a. The first paragraph describes the "severe competition for the means of support." This eliminates those less suited to survive.
2. c. The first sentence of the second paragraph discusses this.
3. e. The last sentence states this.
4. a.

page 49, Huxley
1. c. See paragraph 6, lines 3–7.
2. e. The second paragraph refers to the "common sense of . . . mankind."
3. a. Refer to the fourth paragraph.
4. b. This is discussed in the last sentence.

page 53, Huxley
1. d. The last sentence of the first paragraph concludes that people are "quite wrong" in believing scientific thought is beyond them.
2. a. See lines 8–13.
3. b. The first paragraph discusses this.
4. c. The induction example given is a person concluding that since two hard, green apples are sour, all hard, green apples must be sour.
5. a. The last sentence of the fourth paragraph says that when performing deduction, you have "reasoned out the special conclusion of the *particular* case."

page 56, Durkheim
1. b. The third from the last sentence states that "most of our ideas and tendencies . . . come from outside . . ."
2. a. See lines 5–9.
3. a. This is stated in lines 2–4.
4. d.

page 59, Malthus
1. b. The first sentence states this.
2. e. In the second sentence of the second paragraph, he states that population can never increase without the "food necessary to support it."
3. b.
4. d.

page 62, Freud

1. a. See lines 10–11.
2. d. See line 3.
3. b.
4. c. The last paragraph discusses this.

Humanities

page 67, Keats

1. d. The sonnet was defined earlier as "a fourteen line lyric poem with rigid rhyme scheme and organization."
2. a. He describes the city as a "jumbled heap/Of murky buildings."
3. b. ". . . . If I must with thee dwell . . ." expresses this.
4. c. This is expressed in the last two lines.
5. c. The entire poem is addressed to solitude.

page 70, Wilde

1. b. The other answers do not apply. Their obsession with beauty—even its negative features— suggests that beautiful is what they would like to be.
2. a. The second paragraph states, "The ugly and the stupid have the best of it in this world."
3. e. See lines 2–3.
4. a. See paragraph 2, lines 6–12.

page 73, Tolstoy

1. c. See lines 4–5.
2. a. The anonymous narrator knows all that goes on and offers commentary.
3. d. This is the only sign of wealth not mentioned.
4. d. This is referred to in the second to last sentence.

page 75, Austen

1. a. This is stated in the first two sentences.
2. e. The first sentence of the second paragraph states this.
3. a. Refer to the last paragraph.
4. b.

page 76, Santayana

1. a. He refers to knowledge as a torch that can only light our pathway "but one step ahead."
2. c. A metaphor, as defined earlier, is "an implied comparison."
3. a. Columbus found the New World but "had no chart."

4. d. A paradox is "an apparently self-contradictory statement," as defined earlier.
5. b.

page 79, Dickinson

1. a. Refer to the last two lines.
2. d. The water "lives so far"; the grass "does not appear afraid"; and the sedge "stands next to the sea."
3. b. The bottom of an abyss, like the bottom of a well, is not visible.
4. c. Throughout, the speaker expresses fear and wonder at the mystery of the well. The more she thinks about it, the less confident she feels.

page 81, Dickens

1. b.
2. a. Some clues are the words "wretched," "pompously," and "gorging."
3. a. The focus of the passage is unfairness.
4. c. Pumblechook treats the boy like an object; one could assume that this is how he would treat other students.

page 84, Hawthorne

1. c.
2. a. He admonishes them to "tremble also at each other!"
3. e.
4. a.

page 87, Eliot

1. b. See lines 2–4.
2. c. See line 4 of the second paragraph.
3. e. It is honest because the description is straightforward, understanding because the passage explains why Casaubon feels as he does, and ironic because the narrator clearly does not feel sorry for a man who thinks his wife should see only his good points.
4. c. Refer to the last sentence.

page 89, Poe

1. a. He sets up this relationship in the first paragraph.
2. b. "but the true artist will tone them down"
3. b. "Most readily attainable" indicates there are other sources of beauty.
4. a. He never argues the case for beauty. The other answers don't reflect his thinking.